MW01222552

Cook Islands Travel Guide.

Vacation and Honeymoon Guide

Author
Jesse Russell

Publisher:
SONITTEC LTD
College House, 2nd
Floor
17 King Edwards
Road,
Ruislip
London
HA4 7AE

Table of Content

Summary 1

About Cook Islands 11

Cook Islands Introduction 11

Country guide 14

Sightseeing.. 14

Cities and regions 19

Aitutaki Island... 19

Guide to Aitutaki Island 19

Family trip with kids 24

Culture: sights to visit....................................... 29

Attractions & nightlife 33

Cuisine & restaurants 38

Traditions & lifestyle 44

Accommodation.. 49

Shopping in Aitutaki Island 53

Rarotonga.. 58

Guide to Rarotonga... 58

Beaches of Rarotonga 63

Culture: sights to visit....................................... 67

Attractions & nightlife 69

Cuisine & restaurants 72

Traditions & lifestyle 74

Accommodation.. 77

Tips for tourists 80

The Land.. 83

Relief and drainage 83

Soils 85

Climate 86

Plant and animal life... 87

The People 89

Ethnic groups and languages 89

Religion.. 90

Settlement patterns 90

Demographic trends...90

The Economy..91

Agriculture and fishing 92

Resources and power..92

Manufacturing and trade 93

Services, finance, and taxation 93

Transportation 94

Government And Society..94

Constitutional framework 95

Health and welfare..96

Education...96

Cultural Life 97

History 99

Early cook islands society 100

European explorers..103

Missionaries...104

Disease, population decline & slave traders..............107

Protectorate, annexation & independence...............109

Post-independence politics 110

Financial woes 112

Recent history...113

Rarotonga Island..115

Summary

How Traveling Can Broaden Your Perspective

Cook Islands Guide: You may not need a lot of convincing when it comes to finding a reason to travel especially when considering a trip to a foreign country. Exploring the world, seeing new places, and learning about new cultures are just a few of the benefits of traveling. There is value to exploring someplace new and combating the stress of getting out of your comfort zone.

Traveling should be looked at as a journey for personal growth, mental health, and spiritual enlightenment. Taking the time to travel to a new place can both literally and figuratively open your eyes to things you have never seen before. These new experiences allow you to get to know yourself in ways you can't if you stay in the same place.

✓ Traveling is wonderful in so many ways:

✓ You can indulge your sense of wanderlust.

✓ You experience different cultures.

✓ Your taste buds get to experience unique foods.

✓ You meet all different kinds of people.

As you grow older, your mind evolves and expands to adapt to the new information you receive. Traveling to a new destination is similar in this way, but the learning process occurs at a faster rate. Traveling thrusts you into the unknown and delivers you with a bounty of new information and ideas. The expansion of your mind is one of the greatest benefits of travel. Keep reading to learn six more benefits of traveling.

> Discover Your Purpose: Feeling as though you have a purpose in life is more important than many people realize. A purpose connects you to something bigger than yourself and keeps you moving forward. Your purpose in life can change suddenly and fluidly as you enter new stages in becoming who you are. With each new stage in life, there comes new goals and callings. Traveling can help open your eyes to a new life direction. You may be wandering down a path unaware of where you will end up. Seeing new places and meeting new people can help you break from that path and discover what your true purpose is.

Traveling is an excellent remedy for when you feel you need to refocus on your purpose and goals, or re-evaluate your life path. There is no better time to open your eyes than when your life seems to be out of focus and in need of redirection. You might just be surprised by what you discover and find a new sense of life purpose how traveling changes you.

Traveling is a way to discover parts of yourself that you never knew existed. While traveling, you have no choice but to deal with unexpected situations. For example, how you may typically handle a problem at home might be a completely unacceptable approach when you are in an unfamiliar place without all of the comforts and conveniences of home.

> Be Aware of Your Blessings: When you travel to a new destination, your eyes are opened to new

standards, and, you become more aware of all the blessings and privileges you have been given. It is easy to forget what you do have and only focus on what is missing from your life. Traveling can help put things back into perspective and re-center your priorities on what truly matters.

Consider traveling through an area that has no electricity or running water if you come from a place where cold bottled water is easily accessible and nearly anything you want can be delivered to your door in less than an hour. These are two completely different worlds and ways of living. For people who experience a more privileged quality of life, seeing others who live in drastically different situations can help you appreciate what you have and spark an interest for you to lend support to people living elsewhere.

> Find Truth: There's concept, and then there's experience. You can know things from reading them online and listening to a lecture, but to experience something in person is different.

Traveling can help open your eyes to the true kindness and goodness of humanity. There is a myth that when you travel you are on your own, but that simply is not the case. The welcoming attitude and overwhelming hospitality that people give to travelers may be one of the most surprising truths about traveling. Beyond that, you have the whole world to learn about with every place you discover, through every person you meet and every culture you experience.

> Expand Your Mind: A key benefit of traveling, or taking the opportunity to explore on a vacation, is being given the opportunity to expand your mind in ways you can't imagine. If

you can allow yourself to travel with an open mind and accept the new experiences and adventures around you, you give your mind the chance to see the world from a new perspective.

Think of it as a spiritual and intellectual enlightenment. You never stop being curious and should always seek out education whenever possible throughout your life. You are doing a disservice to yourself if you choose to close yourself off from the world. It is not always easy to let new ideas in, especially when they are in direct contrast with what you may believe. You have everything you need to grow, you just have to allow yourself to do it.

> Connect to Others: It's easy to forget how similar you are to others, regardless of where you come from, what your background is, or how much money you have. At the end of the day,

human beings share more in common with one another than they may choose to admit. When taking a trip to a different country, you may have learned to cast aside what is different and unusual because from the outside, others may not look or act alike. But if you give yourself a chance, you may be surprised to find how minimal and superficial these differences are.

As you notice how you share similar needs, your perspective of your home expands, you become friends with people from different backgrounds and cultures, you realize how everyone is connected. This state of awareness is a jump in consciousness that can help you experience a world-centric view of consciousness more expansive and aware.

> Break Out of Your Shell: Without a doubt, one of the benefits of traveling is that it forces you to

step out of your bubble, which can provide you with many emotional health benefits. Yes, it may be uncomfortable and scary to break away from your daily routine, but the rewards are worth it. What you gain in experience and knowledge may outweigh any amount of doubt or apprehension you had before embarking on your journey. Travel also helps you to self-reflect and dig deep into who you are as a person.

Something magical happens when people are put in new situations than they are normally faced with in their everyday life, as behavior becomes more raw and real as a result of being out of your conditioned environment. This not-so-subtle push into the world helps you to become more open and comfortable expressing yourself without the worry of feeling judged.

> See the Big Picture: Life is a limited gift. You must choose to make the most of each day. As you travel and experience more of the world, you may be struck with gratitude and appreciation for all the places you have enjoyed and people you've shared your travels with. You have the power to take control of your life and can inspire you to start doing more.

About Cook Islands
Cook Islands Introduction

Cook Islands is self-governing island state in free association with New Zealand, located in the South Pacific Ocean. Its 15 small atolls and islands have a total land area comparable to that of a medium-sized city, but they are spread over about 770,000 square miles (2,000,000 square km) of sea an area nearly as large as Greenland. Niue, the westernmost of the islands, is an administratively separate state. The administrative seat is Avarua, on the island of Rarotonga. Area (land only) 91.4 square miles (236.7 square km). Pop. (2011) 14,974.

The Beauty of Cook Islands

Find lazy days dripping with sunshine in the tranquil Cook Islands, 15 sandy freckles in the South Pacific. There are no two ways about it, people come to the Cook Islands for the beaches: pristine ribbons, lapped by sparkling aquamarine waters. For those eager to dive straight in, the Cook Islands' best beaches are at Muri Lagoon and Titikaveka.

Despite covering a vast area, the Cook Islands host a tiny population, and secluded spots are easy to come by. Some islands, such as Rarotonga (where the international airport is situated) and Aitutaki, do feature a number of developed resorts. Mountainous Rarotonga also offers plenty of verdant scenery, should you unlikely though it sounds grow tired of the tropical beach paradise.

Situated between Samoa and French Polynesia, the inhabitants of the Cook Islands are Polynesian, with a proud and interesting culture. Calling themselves the Cook Island Maori, they trace their roots on the southern islands back a millennium to Tahiti and the Marquesas, while Samoans and Togans are responsible for settling the northern islands. The Cook Islanders also hold the tradition that New Zealand Maori migrations originated from their islands.

Named after Captain James Cook, who came here in 1770, the Cook Islands didn't come under British control until 1888. In 1965, the inhabitants chose self-government in free association with New Zealand, which had assumed administrative control over the islands at the turn of the century.

Apart from the interesting culture, it's the natural beauty of the Cook Islands that most captivates visitors. The islands are both volcanic and 'near atolls', which is to say land that's mostly lagoon and edged by islets. You'll find Rarotonga teeming with jungle, while Aitutake is the most photogenic island a true paradise. Expect powdery sand, an abundance of tropical fruits, palm trees and no worries.

Country guide

Sightseeing

Cook Islands sightseeing. Travel guide attractions, sights, nature and touristic places
These tropical islands got their name after Captain Cook, who discovered them in 1770. The Cook Islands become increasingly popular with travelers who seek secluded rest in tropical paradise without busting infrastructure and

hordes of vacationers. The islands are divided into Northern Cook Islands and Southern Cook Islands, with the southern ones being more populated and easily accessible.

Crystal clean water and fantastic underwater life are among the biggest attractions of the islands, so scuba diving and snorkeling are very popular there. The majority of famous diving sites are located around Rarotonga Island. Here divers can see coral reefs, tropical fish, turtles, eagle rays, hammerheads, eels and reef sharks. Divers of all levels are welcome, and larger centers like ones on Muri Beach offer 3 day diving courses for newbies, after which they become certified divers.

Cook Island Christian Church on Rarotonga is one of the most famous architectural landmarks of the islands. The beautiful white-coral building was constructed in 1853. The church is still working and visitors are welcome to attend services. The best way to get acquainted with culture of the Cook Islands is to visit Beachcomber Gallery, which exhibits paintings, jewellery, pearls and other crafts made by local masters. There are workshops behind the building of the gallery, where travelers can buy souvenirs, shell carvings and black-pearl jewellery.

Sir Geoffrey Henry National Culture Centre is a great place to learn more about the colonial past of the islands. The center was founded by Sir Geoffrey Henry, former prime minister of the islands, and consists of six divisions including the National Museum, the National Library, the Anthropology unit, the National Auditorium, Performing Arts and the National Archives.

Cruises have become an essential entertaining activity on the islands. Trips to marvelous lagoons and observation of rich underwater life on glass bottom boats will please both adults and children. The majority of cruises cover Anatakitaki and Atiu caves, which limestone caverns are dotted with stalactites and stalagmites. Other popular destinations include Aitutaki Lagoon and Maina Motu, where travelers will see motu (lagoon islets), coral ridges and rare animals.

History and Entertainment
The first settlers of the Cook Islands were Polynesians forming their settlements here in the 6th century BC. The European discoverers of the islands were Alvaro de Mendana and Pedro Fernandez de Quiros, Spanish navigators who were first to visit the Cook Islands at the turn of the 16th - 17th centuries. Consequently, the

archipelago was also visited by English navigators. At the beginning of the 19th century, the islands were explored by the Russian navigator, Ivan Fyodorovich Kruzenshtern.

The islands gained their present name in the first half of the 19th century. At that time, one of the most significant historical events happened - the building of the first Christian churches. When missionaries came to the islands, there was a long-awaited peace for the natives. Before this, aborigines were in a state of endless war. In the second half of the 19th century, the islands were a British protectorate. In 1901, they became a colony of New Zealand. The Cook Islands gained independence only in 1965. Nowadays, the main guests of the island state are fans of beach entertainments and admirers of undiscovered exotic nature.

Cities and regions

Aitutaki Island

Guide to Aitutaki Island

Sightseeing in Aitutaki Island what to see. Complete travel guide

Aitutaki Island is one of the most comfortable and interesting among the Cook Islands from a tourist point of view; it's is second only to the island of Rarotonga. This picturesque volcanic island has long been chosen by fans of diving, as there are lovely reefs in the immediate vicinity. The island is rich in natural attractions; the main among them is its lagoon. It's noteworthy that the lagoon is shallow; its maximum depth doesn't exceed 3 meters, so that's an ideal place for snorkeling. Divers would have an opportunity to explore the beauty of the barrier reef that surrounds a lagoon.

Despite the fact that the island attracts attention of tourists, it has retained its pristine natural beauty. Its spacious beaches with white sand surrounded by rich exotic vegetation make it perfect for walking and admiring nature. Those who can't imagine their rest without tours would like Aitutaki too. There are several unusual buildings with centuries of history; much of them are concentrated at the south-eastern coast.

Many hundreds of years ago, basalt has been the main building material; amazing building in traditional style constructed of it have perfectly preserved to this day. They are of great value, and each of the buildings has its own unique history.

The largest settlement on the island is the town of Arutanga, the amazingly beautiful architectural complex; it'sstrongly recommended to explore it on foot. Here you can see incredibly amazing houses decorated with elaborately carved woodwork and beautiful stained glass windows. Buildings are constructed in the same style, but each of them has its special charm. The main religious sight is an old church built in 1828. It's believed that this church is the oldest religious building on the Cook Islands.

Fans of natural attractions would enjoy a vast selection of interesting places to explore. It's certainly worth to visit Motu Maina. This amazing miniature archipelago of coral islands is home to rare species of birds. Bird watching is one of the favorite pastimes of tourists. Aitutaki Island is famous for its enchanting events, so many travelers are trying to visit it during festivals. The most striking is Island Nights dedicated to the music and dance traditions of the islanders. Guests of Aitutaki would enjoy beach vacations, get acquainted with natural features of the archipelago and cultural traditions of its indigenous inhabitants.

This picturesque island is an ultimately calm and peaceful place. Aitutaki is an ideal choice for a trouble-free beach vacation. The island is rich in beautiful paths for walking and gorgeous areas for relaxation in an idyllic atmosphere. In recent years, sports infrastructure has appeared on the island's resorts. Nowadays, there are excellent diving centers, surfing schools, and sports gear rental offices. The coast is rich in beautiful small lagoons that are ideal for beginner divers and fans of snorkeling as water is crystal clear there.

Fans of beach recreation should keep in mind that there are not that many comfortable sandy beaches on the island. Coral chips cover a significant part of the coast, and some areas even have coral rocks. It is not comfortable to relax and sunbathe on such beaches without beach gear. The main island is surrounded by numerous tiny uninhabited islands, and vacationers can visit them during boat excursions. During these exciting tours, tourists can see rare animals and various marine creatures.

Aitutaki is particularly popular with romantic couples and newlyweds, who often choose the island to spend holidays together. Local hotels offer numerous services and relaxation programs for couples, including wedding ceremonies right on the coast. Each hotel has luxurious rooms for couples. Lovebirds will be also pleased to find quality spa salons and restaurants. Every year, the range of services and entertainments only grows. Nowadays, it is safe to call Aitutaki a universal resort

Family trip with kids

Family trip to Aitutaki Island with children.
Ideas on where to go with your child

Aitutaki Island is a perfect destination for those families in which kids are obsessed with journeys and always ready to discover something new every day. There are no children infrastructure like theme parks or aquaparks outside local hotels, perhaps just some playgrounds in the capital city. If you plan to also have some time for yourself only, look for those hotels which provide children's rooms and animators. And actually, there is just a few of such hotels.

On the other hand, any kid would fill themselves like Robinson Crusoe here on Aitutaki Island. You just have to go to any desert island e.g. Takutea or Moturakau not far from Aitutaki. Nobody inhabits such small islands, and, what is more, if the weather is nice, you can rent a motorboat and just get there without any troubles. Or you also can have a two-days-excursion to Takutea which includes a sleepover in tents and a cook-house so any child would feel like they participate in a true adventure. Besides, young nature lovers would get interested in it as well as there are lots of diverse exotic birds there.

Aitutaki Island provides a perfects chance for children to try snorkelling. Furthermore, even two-three-years-old children who already can float (with the help of floaties or other inflatable equipment, of course) can take their first lessons. In addition, there is a bunch of reefs that in the ocean area a pretty close to the surface what also allows us to take a closer look at local exotic underwater inhabitants and you don't have to do scuba diving in order to see it. Any child would be so amused to watch all those colourful fishes in real life, not on TV. You can rent a mask and a snorkel in the capital's port.

If your kid is already eight years old, then you can try diving together. English-speaking children have an opportunity to take specialized lessons in any local diving school (as all the lessons are in English). By the end of the courses, kids get a children divers' license which allows them to dive to shallow depths. Moreover, there are pretty much such points here where you can enjoy marine beauty even at such depths. Your children and you could enjoy watching not only tropical fish and various corals but also dolphins and sea turtles in their natural habitat. And, if you're lucky enough, whales too.

If your child prefers to concentrate on just one thing, then you can offer them to try deep-sea fishing. You can rent equipment and a boat and find an instructor too right in the port. Active kids should enjoy taking kite-surfing, sea kayaking or water-skies lessons. Additionally, Aitutaki Island is also especially good for hiking on any distance. Even half-an-hour would be pretty enough to show children some of the local magnificent landscapes or have yourself a half-day hike to explore a rich amount of local tropical birds together with your kids. Young conquerors of the tops have to get to Mount Maungapu.

Novice speleologists should really like the Three Grottos Caves. However, only two of three caves are open for visit presently, the third one is completely caved in for more than ten. So, you can also visit Anatakitaki Cave. But remember that thousands of swiftlets inhabitant the cave, so don't forget to warn your kids about it for them not to get scared of a sudden. Another nice activity is to visit the local botanical garden. It's no that big but defies the imagination by an enormous number of tropical flowers presented in one place.

Kids of any age would probably like the idea of visiting a village of native islanders. One can see how fishermen used to live as well as the Polynesian population's culture. Locals like kids and they would answer all their questions and even meet them with their children with great pleasure. A simple walk around the island's capital is also worth your time. Even though the town is more like a village, 19th-century basalt administration buildings and a church of the year 1828 the very first of all which were built on the Cook Islands have survived up to date. What is more, children might also like to know about the port which was built in the second half of the 20th century and where one can see true fishing boats, leisure boats, casual boats, and canoes.

Culture: sights to visit

Culture of Aitutaki Island. Places to visit old town, temples, theaters, museums and palaces
Aitutaki Island can't boast for its great number of cultural monuments and ancient architectural buildings. On the other hand, people appeared on the island a long time ago. According to scientists, first Polynesian canoes came to the local coats about the 5th century AD or maybe even earlier. Unfortunately, there is no material evidence of what was happening at those days. Polynesians didn't build towns and they didn't need stone houses either. Natives were living in small groups and inhabited simple villages, ate seafood and local fruit. Despite the primitive way of living, descendants of the very first settlers still inhabit the unconquered island. And the fact becomes even more surprising when you remember that the Māori had constantly fought against each other owing to different reasons.

Nevertheless, it's also another reason why there are so little objects of Polynesians' culture here on Aitutaki Island. Moreover, it's rather peculiar that the island's and other adjacent ones' nationals were those who populated New Zeeland, not vice versa.

Europeans found out about the island quite late. It's supposed that William Bligh, captain of the Bounty and then appointed as the Governor of New South Wales, was the first sailor who passed Aitutaki Island. It took place in the 12th century, the year 1789 to be precise.

In addition, Aitutaki Island and the rest of the archipelago were firstly named as the Cook Islands only in the 19th century by famous Russian sailor Adam Johann von Krusenstern. James Cook himself named the territory as Hervey Island. And the locals are lucky on this point. Today, any traveler can visit the traditional Polynesian village that hasn't changed through the last centuries. Englishmen weren't really interested in the island and its neighbouring territories so they didn't even attempt to take the island under control, to build something large here or to make the local population slaves.

You can also travel to the far areas of the island if you'd like to, far from hotels and places of interest, to communicate with the Māori. So, there you can see how people used to fish, build houses and various outbuildings, weave, carve wood, cook, and carry out religious rituals. The Māori don't mind tourists who actually want to find out something new and even can talk to them and tell fascinating stories about their lives. You can also stay at one of the local traditional houses there for a night as a guest, just don't forget to present something to the man of the house or the chief of the tribe it's essential.

There is a rather significant for the religious life of the archipelago construction Christian church(1828), Aratunga. It's the oldest church on the island. It's so important for the locals as it's exactly the place where the first European preaches settled. Conversion to Christianity was quite successful, that is why the church presently is not just one of the local architectural attractions but a pilgrimage object too, especially in the day when the anniversary of the first missionaries' arrival is celebrated. The building is an ideal example of colonial religious architecture. The church has never been reconstructed, so tourists can even now see the original version, just like missionaries planned it to be.

Old town houses and administration buildings are really nice as well, particularly those that are not far from the central square. Most of the are made from basalt. They are not only in the fine condition up to date but also look pretty unusual.

Despite Christianization, people of Aitutaki Island hadn't destroyed other temples and ritual circles and still perform sacred ceremonies there. The main island's harbour which was built just a half-century ago also looks quite peculiar. Modern yachts, casual fish boats, pleasure boats, and traditional colourful canoes share the port.

Attractions & nightlife

City break in Aitutaki Island. Active leisure ideas for Aitutaki Island attractions, recreation and nightlife

Active tourists would especially like Aitutaki Island. There is a great number of opportunities for your fascinating pastime so you definitely won't be bored here. As an example, you can book a short excursion to Takutea which is not far from Aitutaki and designed as a wildlife sanctuary. But remember that one is only able to get there in fine weather. The island has always been uninhabited so you can now see pure jungles with lots of tropics birds' nests. For instance, red-tailed tropicbirds, red-footed boobies, great frigatebirds, sternas, and western reef herons still inhabit the island. Not far from Takutea, there are few large reefs on the surface and that is why it's the ideal place for snorkelling and diving.

You can reach the island from Bounty Bay. The two-three-days excursion includes not just a trip from one point to another and back but also diving in the island's water area, meals, and also provides tents. Aitutaki Island is literally surrounded by dozens of small islands such as

Takutea. You can get to some of these islands, for instance, Moturakau, in a group of tourists. However, it would be easier to just rent a boat or a runabout in case you know how to steer it. Still, don't forget that reefs here a very close to the surface in the local waters, so it's quite risky to sail anywhere on your own.

The atoll in the Aitutaki and its adjacent islands' water areas make it absolutely perfect for snorkellers and divers. You can see hundreds of tropical fish, rays, turtles, starfish, and other inhabitants of the reef here. Multiple solitary bays are the best for snorkelling. However, keep in mind that not the whole Aitutaki's cost is covered with sand as it might seem at first glance. Like, many local bays are covered with layers of coral pieces, so, in case you'd like sunbath there, then it's better to use a hard mat. On the other hand, it's actually really secluded.

And divers would like the place as well. Apart from breath-taking beauty of the reefs, here one can also see dolphins and turtles which are not that afraid of people. And, if you're lucky enough, you might get a chance to see whales too. Moreover, if you don't have a divers' license but extremely want to dive, don't worry. There are several diving schools here on Aitutaki Island where beginners will learn all the peculiarities of this skill. And you can book a diving trip to the point you've got interested in as well as rent equipment if you need it there too. The island will always be a perfect destination for those who like sea kayaking, want to learn surfing, windsurfing, kiteboarding, or water-ski.

Tourists who are highly fond of sea fishing should really appreciate the rich diversity of local underwater species. You can, for example, fish alone from the coast or gather together with friends and rent a runabout and go to the open sea. You can find all the equipment you need in the town port.

If you'd rather simply to relax and enjoy the sun, you can go to Takauroa Beach or Ootu Beach or just to any small bay near the harbour. There are also rather a lot of wild beaches where you can get on a boat by sea with a guide. Nobody would disturb you there, so you can freely enjoy clear water and bright sun.

A romantic type will like the local botanic garden where one can see several hundreds of tropical plants from all over Polynesia. If you're keen on calm walks, then Aitutaki Island is the right place for you too. A two-hours-hike to the pike of Mount Maungapu is definitely worth it. The track goes through amazingly pretty landscapes and then you'll enjoy a wonderful view of the neighbouring islands on the top. If don't really want to make it on your feet, you can drive the one-hour way by car or by bike. In addition, there are lots of tropical birds in the local forests who are not much afraid of people and even let to take a look at them. If you prefer underground landscapes, you should visit the Three Grottos Caves. You can get there by sea or by the cave (where you can see not only stalactites and stalagmites but also find thousands of swiftlets' nests) which is located in the central part of the island.

Cuisine & restaurants

Cuisine of Aitutaki Island for gourmets. Places for dinner best restaurants

Aitutaki Island had been in almost complete isolation for many centuries, so even now you can find here dishes with thousand-years-old recipes. The major change which has happened in the last 100 years is rice adding into the great number of local meals and multiplication of meat dishes. Even though people of the island were eating meat in the past as well, still it used to be served only on major celebrations.

Onions and garlic are now delivered to the island in large quantities indigenous people had never planted it here and so never used in cooking. Since locals got into communication with Europeans, dairy products, beans, cabbage, aubergines, zucchini, tomatoes, and oils started to be brought here and became something especially new for local cooks. Nowadays, all these ingredients are common ingredients for diverse meals on the island. Moreover, new meals appear on the island constantly and they're being created by mixing local traditional recipes with foreign techniques.

Eve those people who are not fond of gastronomic experiments should really try Aitutaki's cuisine. In addition, you don't have to worry about your stomach, the island dishes are not that spicy, hot or sour. The thing you have to be careful about is to make sure that the dish you've chosen is not served raw.

Umukai is definitely worth trying as it's one of the main national dishes in the local traditional cuisine. Basically, it's fish stewed in the earth-oven together with roots and turmeric («renga»). The dish also has a meat-version. Many chefs also like to add onion and garlic, but you can always the traditional recipe in the local remote villages.

Seafood is the base of the cuisine due to the location, so it's not a surprise. If you're looking for something specific, try matu rori. Even though no eggs are used in this dish, it kind of reminds an omelette. The main ingredients are sea cucumber meat, lemon and banana. White crab meat which is usually smashed into puree together with coconut is also rather original. People here eat it raw or fry in hibiscus leaves.

Shellfish grilled on an open fire are extremely tasty. If you're not afraid of eating non-thermally-processed fish then you one hundred percent have to taste ika mata raw tuna or flying fish filet with lime or lemon juice. A salad with fish, which was pickled in seawater and then steamed in order to increase salt concentration, is really tasty too. Then, there is moana-roa mahi mahi white fish filet fried with colocasia and spices.

Papaya (or pawpaw) is the main ingredient for a bunch of local delicacies and it's used of various ripe. What is more, there is a great variety of dishes with sauces made from coconut milk or coconut meat. Fun fact: coconut and papaya meats with lemon and spices are the most popular side dishes or appetizers here on the island. Fried green bananas and colocasia can also be served a nice side dish. Mangos, melons, peaches, and plums are, for instance, often added into salads with coconut chips.

Kuru papa or simply kuru breadfruit fruit is eaten here as a source of carbs. Kuru can not only be an ingredient for salads or appetizers also a base for pies and puddings which are baked in an earth-oven. Tiopu kuru a breadfruit pie with meat is rather tasty as well. Kuru is also sometimes served with punu puakatoro canned beef and pi and ham bean soup. Kuru is also usually added to stewed meat or fish with ginger, turmeric and curry. In addition, colocasia the main local green vegetable is served with major meat dishes.

As for deserts, the really well-known one is poke. It's mostly cooked from bananas boiled in coconut milk or dried or baked ones. However, you can also cool it or simply use any other fruit there are dozens of poke recipes and new ones appear literally every year. Maniota is one more peculiar dessert which is tapioca mashed with coconut milk and then cooked in earth-oven or mixed with starch and baked as a jelly-like pie.

Concerning alcohol, tumunu brewed from oranges and sugar a local kind of beer is definitely worth tasting. Kava is a local non-alcoholic beverage becomes increasingly popular here on the island. Also, you can try local tea which is grown on local plantations.

Traditions & lifestyle

Colors of Aitutaki Island traditions, festivals, mentality and lifestyle

Even though the local population is called the Māori, they actually have not much in common with New Zealand people. About 90% of the islanders are descendants of diverse Polynesian nationalities who came to the island due to the migration process through the Pacific Ocean. Even local Māori Kuki Airani language has loan words from Fijian, Samoan and Tahitian dialects of Polynesia. It's interesting that Aitutaki people call their own language Te Reo Lpukarea meaning «from homeland inherited». Many locals can also speak English because of the great number of tourists and close position to New Zealand. Besides, their speech is quite understandable despite a rather unusual accent.

Islanders still live in communities just like hundred years ago. One community can include several small villages which can also be remote for several kilometres from each other. Indigenous people who have their own complicated chains of family relations and mutual liabilities live in these villages. Men are the head of families but, at the same time, women's opinion is of the same importance, and it's quite a connection with ancient Polynesian matriarchy traditions. Moreover, locals are already used to tourists who come to visit their villages so they actually don't mind telling them about themselves and the way they live.

As you come to one of the local settlements, you should bring gif to the oldest man in the village or to a man of the house. It's better to bring something that definitely wouldn't oblige a person. Locals just can't refuse from any gift and they also have to present something in return. Remember that it's not approved here when somebody raises one's voice during conversations. Beyond that, loud speech or screaming will be taken as manifestations of threats. In addition, take your shoes off as you enter a house. One more taboo here is touching people's heads and especially kids'. Greeting is absolutely casual like in most countries a handshake.

Locals don't approve modern tendency wearing no or partially no clothes. So, if you decided to go somewhere outside touristic zones and beaches, put on, for instance, a shirt and trousers instead of shorts and a T-shirt. Furthermore, one is not allowed to sunbathe topless or naked on crowded beaches.

Despite the fact that the majority of modern inhabitants don't recall that many local legends about the creation of the world, still most people here belong to the Christian religion. The Christian church of the Cook Islands has the greatest number of followers, and, what is more, you can find temples all around the island. If you'd like to, you can visit them even during service. Just remember that you have to act in line and wear right clothes. Women also have to put on a dress or a skirt and a hat.

Nobody is in a hurry on Aitutaki Island. Locals strongly believe that all in good time and just can't understand the European pace of life.

Traditional dance is even now an extremely important part of local culture for natives. It's a significant component of all local events: childbirth, wedding, funeral, and even purchase of an especially expensive property. Many locals also love singing and playing national musical instruments. There are also several church choirs here and almost the whole island enjoys watching their performances.

Various sports competitions are not least popular. Football, rugby, sea kayaking that's what locals do in their free time.

Dogs and roosters are walking around the streets just as a part of country life and many locals will say Kia Orana! to you what means blessing or wishing for good fortune.

The traditional cultural festival takes place the Island Nice on the second week of February. You can see dance and song performances and even visit a market of products made by local craftsmen.

A competition of artistic quilting tivaevae is rather fascinating too. One of the most significant local festivals is Te Maeva Nui a celebration of the local constitution that lasts for 10 days and begins at the closet Friday to the 4th August. Diverse sports competitions, artistic performances and reconstruction of important historical events take place during the festival's program. Locals also greatly celebrate Gospel days. People play the arrival of missionaries on the island. The colourful celebration of Tiaré flowers takes place at the end of November.

Accommodation

Best hotels for short vacation or business trip to Aitutaki Island

Tamanu

Luxury resorts of Aitutaki Island are sure to impress even the most discerning travelers. Tamanu Hotel located at the picturesque beach of the same name is popular among travelers. Its guests live in pretty individual bungalows with traditional roofs of palm fronds; they are located a few steps away from the coast. The hotel complex is surrounded by dense thickets of trees. The recreation area is quite amazing; that's a wooden terrace with panoramic views of the coast. The hotel has its own travel agency arranging enchanting shows every week.

The Aitutaki Lagoon

The upscale hotel The Aitutaki Lagoon , as its name suggests, is located in the beautiful lagoon. The lodge completely occupies a small island with white sand. Part of the bungalows are set on stilts over the water, they all feature excellent technical equipment. The hotel complex offers a wide range of services; it has a luxury spa and a beachfront restaurant with a rich menu. Fans of excursions won't be bored too, as there are interesting daily events here.

Aitutaki Escape

One of the most prestigious hotels on the island is Aitutaki Escape , it offers guests three luxurious villas. All houses are built in keeping with local traditions and have a finish of rare marble. Interior of luxury villas also deserves the highest praise; it's harmoniously complemented by original decoration in traditional style. The hotel is characterized by calm and harmonious atmosphere; fans of sport would like it too. Everybody can rent equipment for scuba diving and other sports activities.

The famous hotel Rino's Ltd is situated to the west of the island. It's ready to offer customers cozy rooms and private bungalows with view of the coast. This attractive hotel with homely atmosphere is perfect for families with children;

its rooms are technically equipped and suitable for long-term accommodation. Just a couple of steps separate the hotel from the coast, were a lot of pleasant surprises are waiting for guests. The beach is equipped with sun loungers and wooden benches, as well as comfortable tables in shade of palm trees making it a perfect place for a picnic.

Paradise Cove

Budget and independent travelers like Paradise Cove Hotel. Its bungalows are literally hidden in dense thickets of tropical plants. Each bungalow has a fully equipped kitchen and a full set of modern appliances. The hotel can be perfect for a vacation with the whole family. There is also beach equipment rental, as well as a great barbecue zone.

Pacific Resort

Discerning travelers should pay attention to the luxury hotel complex Pacific Resort . It's the biggest accommodation place on the island offering customers a large selection of comfortable rooms and private villas. Suites are particularly noteworthy, as all of them have unusual open bathrooms set in a tropical garden. Rich buffet is served in the morning and in the evening; amazing events are arranged in the afternoon. All the hotels located next to the coast of the island are aimed primarily at fans of beach activities. Hotels have their own top-level water sports centers; equipment rentals can be found even in small hotels.

Shopping in Aitutaki Island

Shopping in Aitutaki Island authentic goods, best outlets, malls and boutiques

Aitutaki is a comparatively small island. Here you can find a great variety of souvenirs made by local craftsmen as well as basic necessities. However, if you're aimed at the huge shopping that includes clothes and shoes by famous brands, then you should go to Rarotonga or better make a day or two for a trip to New Zealand. And even if you'll find this kind of stuff on Aitutaki, it will be really expensive and of a little choice.

If you didn't take an insect repellent with, buy one immediately as soon as you can, otherwise you're risking being bitten by anopheles.

The best time for shopping here is Saturday morning. Oddly enough, at that time all the stores here are open.

Euros or American dollars can be accepted only in the major supermarkets, so it's better to change your money into local dollars.

Locals are not used to bargain. An argument concerning price is not a part of a purchasing process here on the island. A seller is meant to sell a product for the price they originally put. There is a possibility that somebody would agree to low a price but it still might happen only in touristic places.

Funnily enough, one of the most popular purchases among tourists who come to the island is a typical souvenir a magnet with Aitutaki Islands' sceneries. Probably it's because many travellers come to the island just for a couple of hours as a part of their Pacific cruise; at the same time, perhaps it's because of New Zealand people who often come here, and they can diverse creations of local craftsmen in the homeland too. Nevertheless, the fact remains magnets depicting Aitutaki views as well as T-shirts and caps are sold here in enormous amount and rather cheap. So, it would be a nice present for relatives or colleagues.

If you're still looking for something that would remind you of the local style, consider to buy a tury. It's a large hand-made blanket made from local plant fibre. Locals sew diverse geometric patterns with ritual meaning or just with the island's views on it and sell to tourists. Still, the local population uses tury at their homes too. A quilt would be another unusual souvenir. It's a highly popular piece of décor here on the island. It's a centuries-old tradition to sew it by hand.

You can find here on Aitutaki a great number of things made from stuff one can find in the sea, what is typical for all seaside territories. Works from corals are especially valued here. Thankfully, there is an atoll here so there is always enough material. Despite the fact that it's a rather trite gift, the local coral works deserve special attention. People create them for many centuries and decorate their houses with it or present to their close ones, as they've learned how to make it in perfection. Besides, here you can also buy nice coral, shell and semi-precious gems necklaces, they are pretty cheap and look really great.

If you like local fashion, you can also buy a flamboyant dress or a light colourful man shirt. Locals also love straw hats and make them here on the island as well. You can buy not just straw hats but also straw mats, small boxes or hot pads here on Aitutaki Island. There are also many wood masters who create and sell functional stuff like furniture and various boxes as well as just decorations carved animal figures, masks depicting spirits or wooden panels.

Moreover, you can also buy yourself talismans of any kind. Locals are quite superstitious despite Christianization and still create different talismans as protection from evil spirits and misfortunes. A pack of local coffee would be a universal souvenir. It's of high quality and grown right here on the island and, unfortunately, is nor exported anywhere outside the Cook Islands. Breadfruit crisps and local tropical fruit would be a marvellous present. You can also bring home a bottle of tumunu a citrus alcoholic beverage with sugar and yeast or non-alcoholic kava.

Rarotonga

Guide to Rarotonga

Sightseeing in Rarotonga what to see.
Complete travel guide

Rarotonga is one of the youngest lands among the Cook Islands. Narrow coastline surrounded by trees, majestic mountains and deep gorges -

all this natural splendor never ceases to attract travelers from different countries. At first glance, the island may seem quite unexplored and uninhabited, but its territory has well-developed tourist infrastructure.

Tourists are offered a large variety of tours, during which they could learn about the culture of Polynesian people, visit picturesque lagoons and stroll through the tropical forests, as well as scuba dive and admire the beauty of the underwater world. Fans of extreme activities can take a helicopter and enjoy the breathtaking view of the island with a bird's-eye view.

Unlike artificial islands, Rarotonga is literally drenched with mighty energy of wildlife. The island is occupied with coconut and citrus groves, vines and ferns jungle; in local forests you can find rare plants. The man wasn't able to create such magnificence with his hands.

The island was long chosen by fans of deep sea fishing. Fishers harvest marlin, barracuda, tuna and other precious breeds of fish. In every part of the island you can find attractive restaurants and shops; local civilization literally borders with dense jungle.

The capital of the island is the town of Avarua. Its name literally translates as 'two harbors.' Back in 1992, it was a humble port city, but after the past festival of Maire Nui it started to develop. Today is a large tourist center. Amazing avenues and streets buried in the greenery, unique architectural constructions built in the best traditions of Polynesia and the lovely green hills on the horizon - this is how Avarua looks like. The main tourist attraction is a group of trees called

Seven-In-One-Coconut-Tree. Palm trees form a perfect circle; a lot of interesting stories are associated with this natural landmark. Rarotonga also features several medieval buildings, churches and ancient cemeteries. Local museums represent a rich collection of historical and archaeological exhibits, as well as handicrafts and national costumes.

Rarotonga Island is a perfect place for diving. There are a lot of beautiful coral reefs near it. Here, you can see rare species of exotic fish and other sea dwellers, admire underwater caves and other wonderful attractions. Fishing is also very popular with the guests of the island. Local water sports centers regularly organize trips to popular fishing docks. There is another pleasant surprise for fans of fishing. After recreation, they can take their catch to one of the multiple restaurants where experienced chefs will cook seafood for them.

Nature admirers and fans of active holidays should certainly visit the Cocopat Amusement Park. It was created specially for tourists. There are a lot of sportsgrounds and recreation areas in this picturesque place. Here, you can play golf, have a wonderful picnic among exotic plants, and make use of the services offered by water sports centers. In the park, there are many beautiful places for walks and special playgrounds for children. For vacationers' convenience, there are several restaurants and sports equipment rental centers in the territory of the park.

Fans of exciting sightseeing tours won't be disappointed too. They can see wonderful Stone Papeyha. It is located in the capital and is a monument that reminds the locals of the important historical event. The stone was named after the first missionary reaching the archipelago and preaching the Christian teaching. The beautiful monument cut in the stone in honor of this event is a real pride for the locals now. In the capital, there is an old Christian church. It was built in 1849 and is the first church on the Cook Islands.

It will be interesting for fans of event tourism to visit the island in February. The traditional Dance and Culture Festival is held at this time here. It lasts for a week. During the festival, you can witness music and dance groups' performances and see the works of local craftsmen and artists. At the festival, travelers have also an opportunity to buy a lot of unique gifts and take part in interesting entertainments.

Beaches of Rarotonga

Vacation on Rarotonga beaches hidden bays, top resorts and recreation areas

Rarotonga Island attracts lots of diving and snorkeling fans thanks to a huge selection of amazing coral reefs nearby. Those who prefer sun baths at the picturesque coast would enjoy a number of charming beaches. Amazing Oravaru Beach is the one of the symbols of Rarotonga. It's also among the largest across all Cook Islands' beaches. This massive coast is covered with soft snow-white sand contrasting with nearby exotic wilds and deep blue water. This beach lacks any equipment and most of its visitors are divers. Lots of colorful fishes in coastal waters are an excellent sight for both experienced and newbie divers. There's also lots of hiking routes around, while nearby green hills provide excellent panoramic view over surrounding area.

Oneroa Beach is another interesting choice; it's among the most beautiful and popular on the island. This quiet bay is a good option for family vacation and this sand beach is widely regarded after its quiet atmosphere and beautiful landscapes. Coastal waters are full of fish and attract lots of fishermen. The place is also popular among photographers thanks to excellent shot opportunities.

Romantic natures will surely like Avaavaroa beach. This tiny coast is surrounded with thick palm wilds sometimes almost touching the waterline. Thanks to that sunshades aren't necessary at the beach. Despite its popularity, Avaavaroa is never crowded. Tikioki is way livelier and busy thanks to major roadways passing nearby. However, due to beach size it's not too difficult to find comfortable place to rest. Tikioki is a good choice for everyone from water sports fans to families and those who like to take sun baths in peaceful places.

Charming Muri beach is for reason regarded as the most sough-after place for rest on Rarotonga. The beach is very quiet and simply amazing surrounded with high green hills and thick tropical wilds. There are also a number of luxurious hotels nearby. Calm lagoon is the perfect choice for vacation with children and also for those who like to rest in comfort.

Black Rock Beach is among the most interesting places to rest. This picturesque beach is a good call for fans of water activities and hiking enthusiasts thanks to lots of natural landmarks around. Huge black rocks of unusual forms scattered all across the coast are in fact solidified lava. Surprisingly the only evidence of past volcano eruptions and entire beach is covered with snow-white sand. Another attractive place is Ngatangiia bay. It's known after its harbor station and offers both sea excursion opportunities and excellent seascape views.

Culture: sights to visit

Culture of Rarotonga. Places to visit old town, temples, theaters, museums and palaces
Rarotonga Island is the good choice for those who like sports and beaches, but also for excursions fans. There are lots of places of interest spread through scenic towns and villages. The Cook Islands Library and Museum Society is the one of the most interesting places. There is an extensive cultural center with various exhibitions in the capital city of Avarua. The library holds lots of book; there is also an exhibition of traditional crafts, unique show-pieces and photographs.

Traffic Circle is the most beautiful part of the city; that is where one of the island symbols is located. That's the Seven-In-One-Coconut-Tree unique palms. They form a precise ring; numerous tales and legends are associated with them. According to one of them, all seven trees grew up from a single seed. Another landmark is the church built in 1853. There is also a number of true Polynesian buildings that are over more than one hundred years old.

Arorangi village, the very first missionary settlement on Rarotonga, is located at the west coast. This colorful village has managed to survive to these days almost intact; it offers lots of interesting buildings to see, including the island's most important religious landmark Cook Islands Christian Church, also known as CICC. Church was built in the mid19th century; it is the burial place of missionary Papeih, who introduced Christianity to island tribes.

Next to Arorange there is the Cultural Village, the huge open air ethnographic museum. There tourists can learn a lot about local crafts and cuisine, purchase unique hand-made souvenirs and taste national meals. Takitumu area on the south of Rarotonga is the excellent place for those who like to walk around historical areas. There they can visit beautiful Pa' palace and Arai Te Tonga royal court ruins. The latest are sacred for local citizens.

Attractions & nightlife

City break in Rarotonga. Active leisure ideas for Rarotonga attractions, recreation and nightlife Rarotonga is the island with wide beaches and picturesque nature, various entertainment and fitness centers, interesting shops and restaurants. Titikaveke beach is the most popular on the island. That's a lovely quiet place surrounded by palm bushes providing an excellent sun cover. The beach is very long making it easy to find sole place to rest.

Another appealing place is the Muri Lagoon beach that is extremely popular among divers. Lots of colorful fishes, starfishes and other underwater dwellers can be seen close to the shore. This calm and well-tended beach is an excellent place to rest in a hot sunny day. Lots of diving centers offer their services to fans of diving; there are also diving schools, if you are new to diving.

Cocoputt entertainment park is an excellent place to take a break, especially if to travel with your family. Lots of picnic areas are set up inside the park along with sports grounds and restaurants. Visitors can take a walk around winding pathways or play golf and taste local treats.

Maire Nui botanical garden is an excellent place to meet local flora and fauna. The garden is nicely designed; it offers a huge collection of flowers. There are also comfortable cafes for tired visitors. LEK Rarotonge center is the place to visit for fans active leisure. It offers lots of various equipment and sports activities including diving and surfing.

Lots of attractive shops and markets are also worth mentioning. The most popular is the Punanga Nui market located at the island' capital town. Lots of traditional goods are sold there, including clothes, foot wear and souvenirs. Quite often there are entertainment shows at the market.

Cuisine & restaurants

Cuisine of Rarotonga for gourmets. Places for dinner best restaurants

Rarotonga amazes gourmets and those who prefer exotic dishes. The isolation of the island was the main reason for special culinary traditions to appear. Recipes of many local treats have remained unchanged for more than one hundred years. One of the main innovations of the national cuisine is using rice and meat, as a hundred years ago meat has been used exclusively for cooking holiday treats.

Rice appeared on the island relatively recently; today it is considered an important component of many classic treats and everyday meals. National cuisine would appeal to seafood lovers and vegetarians, as numerous interesting vegetable dishes are cooked here. Cabbage and zucchini, eggplant and rice are main components of local dishes. Chefs cook a lot of interesting and savory treats of these simple and well-known ingredients.

There is also the national drink here, a special kind of malt beer called Tutunu. A typical example of an old national dish is umukai. Like many years ago, this special dish is cooked in a mud stove. Umukai is steamed seafood with vegetables. Several decades ago, indigenous people began to invent different kinds of umukai; it was the time, when locals started cooking meat and adding seasonings such as garlic and onions.

Mat Rory is the most unusual among exotic treats; that's meat of sea cucumber or trepang fried with a special variety of green bananas. The taste of the dish is just amazing. Local chefs cook very interesting dishes of white crabs, which are also considered delicacies. Meat is pounded, then mixed with coconut and fried in a little with hibiscus leaves. Fans of the exotic can enjoy even more original dish, raw crab meat dressed with lemon juice.

Another specific treat is salted fish; locals salt it right in seawater. Such fish can be served as an independent course and as a supplement to other treats. Local restaurants serve exotic fruits as desserts; roasted breadfruit cause a great interest among foreign visitors.

Traditions & lifestyle

Colors of Rarotonga traditions, festivals, mentality and lifestyle

Rarotonga is the amazingly beautiful and charming island with interesting cultural traditions. Music and dance have become indispensable attributes of everyday life. The islanders consider themselves the best dancers of Oceania and not without a reason. Travelers who wish to get acquainted with local culture and traditions have to visit the island during the second half of April, when a festival of dance Te Mire Ura takes place. It is attended by the best dance groups of the Cook Islands; the festival is accompanied by grandiose performances and music concerts. During the last day of the festival, the best dancers of the year are chosen. The event is finished by the grand concert.

Traditional Song-Quest music festival is held in July; it is attended by the best performers. This music festival lasts for five weeks and visitors of the island can attend concerts and interesting entertainment every day. One of the most popular national holidays is Te Maeva Nui Festival, the Constitution Day. The holiday is dedicated to the important historical event, the attainment of independence. Lush festivities last for 10 days; the festival is held in early August.

The festival program is very rich and diverse, so its guests can witness exciting sports and colorful street performances, concerts and a fair. During the festival, there are interesting excursions and cultural events dedicated to the history and traditions of islands.

The main religious holiday is Nuku or Gospel Day. Each year, the date of the holiday varies, so tourists wishing to get acquainted with religious traditions of the island have to specify the date in advance. November has always been associated with colorful Tiare or Floral festival; it is visited by florists from different countries. The festival is complemented by very interesting exhibitions and competitions; skilled florists compete in designing landscape compositions and facades of buildings and their works look simply irresistible. At each festival foreigners will feel welcomed, as Rarotonga has very welcoming and friendly atmosphere.

Accommodation

Best hotels for short vacation or business trip to Rarotonga
Muri Beach Club
Luxurious resort hotels represent one of the most appealing features of Rarotonga. Muri Beach Club is among leaders of local hospitality services. The hotel occupies charming Muri lagoon that is one of the most beautiful places on the island. That's an excellent choice for active tourists thanks to multiple water sports and sight-seeing options. There is a great restaurant for gourmets, and stylish lounge offers its guests a wide selection of exotic cocktails. Tropical

forests around the hotel make it even more appealing.

Club RaroClub Raro
beach hotel is located in the capital town that shares name with the island itself. The hotel offers its guests simple, but functional rooms decorated in bright colors. Prices are among the advantages of Club Raro. The hotel is situated just a few steps away from scenic coastline; there is an amazing swimming pool and a bar on its territory. The charming hotel restaurant offers the most popular local dishes.

Te Manava Luxury Villas & Spa
Demanding tourists should pay attention to Te Manava Luxury Villas & Spa complex boasting one of the best day spas on the island. The hotel offers its guests fully equipped private villas decorated according to national traditions. There's also an excellent water sports center for

active tourists. Travelers interested in local traditions and culture will be surprised with daily entertainment events and shows.

Sanctuary RarotongaSanctuary Rarotonga
is among the best hotels on the island. Located next to Aroa Lagoon, it offers its services only to adult tourists. There's an excellent wellness center with open air cabins surrounded with exotic plants. The hotel occupies the beautiful villa in traditional style decorated with natural materials.

The Rarotongan Beach Resort & Spa
Luxurious The Rarotongan Beach Resort & Spa is situated at the picturesque private beach and thus is very popular among fans of water activities and travelers with kids. Younger tourists will enjoy the excellent club with daily entertainment events and various courses. Demanding travelers love this hotel because of

its luxurious day spa with open-air cabins, while theme evenings would be excellent entertainment for every guest.

Little Polynesian ResortLittle Polynesian Resort located in Titikaveka bay is another interesting choice. The hotel offers its guest private villas and fully equipped rooms situated at the scenic tropical garden few steps away from the beautiful beach. There's unusual open bathroom at some villas. Homelike welcoming atmosphere of the hotel will be an excellent addition to vacations there.

Tips for tourists

Preparing your trip to Rarotonga: advices & hints things to do and to obey

1. The rainy season is from November to April; the lowest precipitation is from May to October. In other months, sudden tropical storms are also

possible, but they are usually short-lived and, thus, won't spoil the holiday program.

2. Two currencies run on the island; those are New Zealand dollar and Cook Islands dollar. Exchange rate is the same; the main difference between currencies is that the latest isn't used outside of the islands. Travelers can exchange currency at a local bank, but it would be more profitable to do that in their home country before departing.

3. Banks and other government agencies are open from 9:00 am to 3:00 pm from Monday to Thursday; Friday is a longer working day. Some big banks may also be open on Saturday; however, Sunday is the common day off.

4. Vacationers have to consider that isn't acceptable to leave a tip for waiters, taxi drivers and other service personnel. If you want to thank

a taxi driver or waiter, you can round the resulting amount up to any sum.

5. Going shopping it's also worth considering that bargaining is not accepted at local markets and shops. It is strongly advised to stock up a sufficient number of notes and coins of small denomination, as it will be easier to pay off the sellers.

6. Tourists who plan to purchase items of mother-of-pearl, coral or skin are sure to fill out the supporting documentation. You are not recommended to buy these items at the open market, as bill of sale is provided by authorized shops only.

7. Mains voltage is 220 V; hotels and inns use sockets of New Zealand standard. Some large hotels may equip their ooms with other types of

sockets, but it's better to take adapters for electrical appliances in advance.

8. The best time to go shopping is Saturday morning. At this time, all markets and shops are working; they gradually begin to close in the afternoon. On Sunday, on the contrary, most of the shops don't work.

9. You can move around the island by bus; it runs along the coast from early morning to late in the evening. The timetable isn't accurate, but usually the range between buses is no more than an hour.

The Land

Relief and drainage

Each island is the top of one or more volcanoes, but only on the largest islands do the plugs and craters of now-extinct volcanoes still dominate the skyline; the highest of these rises to 2,139 feet (652 metres) at Te Manga, on Rarotonga, an island only 4 miles (6 km) wide. Many of the other islands of the southern group (Aitutaki, Atiu, Mangaia, Manuae, Mauke, Mitiaro, Palmerston, and Takutea) show various combinations of atoll and high-island formation. In the northern group (Manihiki, Nassau, Penrhyn, Pukapuka, Rakahanga, and Suwarrow), all except Nassau are atolls, narrow and low-lying sandbanks resting on circular reefs around lagoons rich in marine life.

Because the land areas are so small, there are no rivers, and only the largest islands have even small streams. There are small freshwater lakes on the high islands of Mangaia, Atiu, and Mitiaro; saltwater lagoons inside all the atolls; and fringing lagoons between most islands and their outer reefs. The rain that falls on the atolls permeates the island coraland is naturally stored in a lens-shaped layer above the heavier salt water. The islanders must rely on wells and rainwater storage tanks to conserve their limited sources of water.

Soils

Soils on the low-lying atolls are very limited in depth and quality. Most of the high island of Rarotonga is ruggedly mountainous, with narrow valleys having small but fertile pockets of soil. The coast consists of *makatea*, or upraised coral reef, of limited fertility. Between the mountains and the coast, however, is a ring of fertile volcanic soil. On the other high islands, much of the area is likewise taken up by eroded central slopes encircled by *makatea*, but again there are areas of fertile soil between. The problem of erosion has been greatly accentuated by the planting of pineapples and other export crops on soils that, in the long term, are too fragile for plantation farming.

Climate

All the islands lie within the tropics, though the southernmost just barely so. Because the Cook Islands are small, mid-ocean islands swept by the southeast trade winds, temperatures are generally moderate. Mean annual temperatures on the southern island of Rarotonga are in the mid-70s F (about 24 °C), but on the northernmost island of Penrhyn they are in the low 80s F (about 28 °C).

Seasons are not clearly differentiated. The English terms *summer*, *winter*, *spring*, and *autumn* are used, but Cook Islanders also recognize the traditional local patterns of prevailing winds, rainfall, and temperature. Precipitation, though erratic over the years, tends to be uniform across the various islands. It averages about 80 inches (2,000 mm) on Rarotonga, though with considerable difference between the windward and leeward sides of the central mountains; precipitation is slightly lower on Aitutaki and slightly higher on Penrhyn.

A spectacular climatic hazard is the occurrence of tropical cyclones (locally called typhoons), which strike with destructive force between December and March about once or twice every 10 years. Less spectacular but at times equally destructive of agriculture are droughts, to which the northern group of islands is more vulnerable than the southern.

Plant and animal life

Only a limited range of plant life thrives in the north, with coconuts and pandanus being predominant. On the fertile areas of the southern islands, a wide range of tropical fruits and vegetables flourishes. Indigenous species include taro, yams, bananas, breadfruit, and sweet potatoes. Introduced species in many cases grown for export include citrus fruits, tomatoes, pineapples, papayas, beans, and zucchini.

The original Polynesian settlers brought with them pigs, dogs, chickens, and a type of small rat. Those are still the main fauna, though a few goats, horses, and other animals have also been introduced. Some native birds became extinct in the 19th century after Europeans introduced cats. The *kakerori*, or Rarotongan flycatcher, an attractive tiny bird unique to Rarotonga, had been reduced by the early 1990s to about 30 breeding pairs. By the early 21st century, however, efforts by a small group of conservationists and landowners had succeeded in increasing the *kakerori* population to a viable level again. In 2012 the government announced plans to create a protected marine park encompassing the area around the southern islands, with an area of more than 400,000 square miles (1,000,000 square km).

The People

Ethnic groups and languages

With the exception of the inhabitants of isolated Pukapuka, who are of predominantly Samoan and Tongan descent, almost all Cook Islanders have mixed Polynesian ancestry. Intermarriage with European, Chinese, and African settlers was common in the early 19th century. There are two main indigenous Polynesian languages, one for the island of Pukapuka and the other (with dialectal variations) for all other islands. The latter, known as Cook Islands Maori, is an official language, as is English.

Religion

Christian denominations account for nearly all religious affiliation. Just over half of the population belongs to the Cook Islands Christian (Congregational) Church. Roman Catholicism, Anglicanism, Seventh-day Adventism, and Bahā'ī have smaller numbers of adherents.

Settlement patterns

Most Cook Islanders live in villages, though some people (on Rarotonga particularly) live on their farms. The largest settlement is Avarua. The former indigenous houses of thatch and timber have been almost totally replaced by homes of cement and timber with iron roofs.

Demographic trends

Life expectancy at birth is above 70 years for males and about 75 years for females. Natural increase is offset by emigration to New Zealand and Australia, though expatriates are counted among the Cook Islands' official population, of which they constitute almost half. Today more than twice as many persons of Cook Islands ancestry live in New Zealand than in the islands themselves.

More than nine-tenths of the Cook Islands' population is native-born. The main nonindigenous population is of European origin by way of New Zealand. There is considerable internal migration from the smaller islands to Rarotonga, the most populous island, where there is generally full employment.

The Economy

Agriculture and fishing

Agricultural production consists primarily of small farming, either for domestic consumption or for shipment to New Zealand. Cassava, sweet potatoes, and other roots and tubers are the principal crops. Most commercial fishing is done by Taiwanese, South Korean, and Japanese vessels operating out of American Samoa, but there is widespread fishing for domestic consumption. Several species of tuna make up the primary catch.

Resources and power

Phosphate is present on the floor of the Manihiki lagoon, and there are vast deposits of manganese and cobalt and some other metals on the seabed near Manihiki. Exploratory mining operations began there in 1999. Imported fuels are utilized for energy production, though there is some use of solar and wind power.

Manufacturing and trade

The small industrial sector includes clothing and shoe manufacturing and food processing, mainly for export to New Zealand. Cultured pearls and fish are by far the major exports. Machinery of various kinds, minerals and fuels, and food and live animals are significant imports. New Zealand, Australia, and Fiji are the leading sources of imports; major export destinations are Japan, New Zealand, and Australia.

Services, finance, and taxation

The service sector dominates the economy, with tourism the largest single contributor. Visitors come mainly from New Zealand, Australia, the United States, Canada, and Europe. The second largest economic sector is international finance, as the Cook Islands are a major offshore tax haven. Government plays a significant part in the economy and is the largest employer. Taxes are moderate, foreign investment is encouraged, and foreign aid largely from New Zealand makes a significant contribution to the economy. The New Zealand dollar is the monetary unit of the Cook Islands.

Transportation

Each island has a network of roads; a paved road encircles Rarotonga and is served by public buses. Regular service by small aircraft connects all the larger islands. There are ports at Rarotonga (Avatiu), Penrhyn, Mangaia, and Aitutaki, but shipping schedules can be erratic. There is an international airport on Rarotonga.

Government And Society

Constitutional framework

The Cook Islands is a self-governing state. Although New Zealand is nominally responsible for defense and for external affairs, the Cook Islands has nevertheless independently established diplomatic relations and entered into international treaties. The formal head of state is the British monarch, represented by an appointed delegate to the islands; the government of New Zealand also appoints a representative, known as the high commissioner. Day-to-day executive power is vested in a cabinet headed by the prime minister and appointed by the islands' unicameral Parliament.

Parliamentary elections, with universal adult suffrage, are held every four years. The constitution, adopted in 1965, has been amended several times. A council of hereditary leaders, the House of Ariki (High Chiefs), advises the government on traditional matters of landownership, custom, and the like. The two main political parties are the Cook Islands Party and the Democratic Party.

Health and welfare

Free medical services are available from government-owned hospitals or dispensaries on each island. Dental treatment is also free for schoolchildren. Diseases more commonly found in developed countries diabetes, cardiovascular disorders, cirrhosis of the liver are becoming more widespread.

Education

Education is free in government schools and compulsory between ages 5 and 15; some church schools operate in addition to those run by the government. Higher education is provided by a national teachers college and a nursing school, through apprenticeship programs, and through an extension centre of the University of the South Pacific at Avarua. Many overseas scholarships are provided by the government and by overseas donors. The vast majority of the people are literate.

Cultural Life

The government plays an active role in cultural life, particularly in the sponsorship of song and dance festivals for which the islands are renowned. A small library and museum in Avarua provide additional cultural attractions. Owing to tourism and intensive interaction with neighbouring industrialized nations, much international (generally Western) culturehas been incorporated into daily life. Nevertheless, traditional ceremonies, such as that celebrating the first haircut of the favourite son in a family, are as vibrant as ever. The islands' distinctive cuisine draws on the traditions of Europe, China, Fiji, and Tahiti. Christian tradition, some of it a legacy of the English Victorian era, is strongly manifest, and modern American-derived evangelistic services and rituals are common. The major national holiday is Constitution Day, which usually gives rise to a 10-day celebration. A Tiare ("Gardenia") Festival, a parade of floats, and a series of song and dance competitions fill the annual calendar of festivities.

The broadcast media are privately owned, although the government issues licenses. Radio programming is available in English and Maori. Much of the television programming comes from New Zealand. The only daily newspaper, formerly government-owned, was privatized in 1989; other newspapers are published weekly or fortnightly.

History

Cook Islanders are Polynesians: people of the *poly* (many) islands of the South Pacific. They are closely related to the Maoris of New Zealand and Tahiti (Cook Islanders can happily converse with their Maori cousins from overseas, despite differences in vocabulary and dialect).

The Cook Islands were first settled around 1500 years ago by travellers from the Society and Marquesas Islands (now known as French Polynesia). Polynesians had been trekking across much of the South Pacific in huge ocean-going canoes for a couple of millennia before they arrived in the Cooks. The first settlers arrived in Melanesia from Southeast Asia around 2500 BC, before heading on to Fiji, Samoa and Tonga; French Polynesia was then settled somewhere between 200 BC and AD 200. From there, canoes travelled thousands of kilometres in all directions, reaching Rapa Nui (Easter Island), Hawaii, South America, and finally Rarotonga and the Cook Islands in around AD 500.

Early cook islands society

Although written records only began with the arrival of the Europeans, oral history on Rarotonga traces its ancestry back about 1400 years. One of the oldest legends tells the tale of To'i, the great chief who built the Ara Metua (the ancient inland road) on Rarotonga somewhere around the 11th century, suggesting that there was already a sizable population living on the island (probably settlers from present-day French Polynesia). Traditional history, however, begins in the 13th century with the arrival of Tangi'ia and Karika, great chiefs from Tahiti and Samoa, who arrived aboard mighty ocean-going *vaka* (canoes), conquered the resident population, and founded Rarotonga's six main tribes.

Every island in the Cooks was ruled by several *ariki* (high chiefs). Beneath the *ariki* were *mataiapo* (chiefs) and *rangatira* (sub-chiefs). Land was divided into sections called *tapere,* each governed by one or more *mataiapo,* and home to a large extended family who used the land to build houses, farm crops and raise livestock. Each tribe had its own *marae* (sacred meeting places) and worshipped specific gods. The *koutu* was the most important meeting place of all - it was the official seat of a ruling *ariki,* and the place where the main sacrifices, offerings and annual feasts were made.

A chief's authority depended on his *mana* - a complex term signifying not just physical or hereditary power, but also confidence, victory, prestige, knowledge, spirituality and all-round star quality. *Mana ariki* was the hereditary power of a chief; *mana atua* was the divine authority of the priest; and *mana tutara* was the ruling power of a *mataiapo*. *Mana* could be gained as well as lost; great deeds in battle and cowardly acts could all affect a person's *mana,* and the way he was regarded by the tribe.

Ta'unga (literally 'experts') were also important figures. There were *ta'unga* in many fields, including woodcarving, agriculture, medicine, canoe-making and navigation. The *tumu korero* (speaker) was responsible for memorising tribal history and genealogy, but the most powerful *ta'unga* was the high priest, who was seen as the main bridge between the people and the spirits of the gods and ancestors. The high priest could declare certain acts or places *tapu* (forbidden), either by order of the gods or the *ariki;* the chief would decide when *tapu* had been violated and what the punishment would be (generally it was likely to be fairly unpleasant).

Like their modern-day descendants, early Cook Islanders never passed up the opportunity for a party. There were elaborate ceremonies for all kinds of occasions - coming-of-age ceremonies, marriages, deaths, harvest festivals and victories in battle - so the islanders had plenty of opportunity to perfect their song and dance routines.

European explorers

The Cook Islands had over a thousand years to develop its distinctive culture and customs before any Europeans finally pitched up. The first Europeans to sight the islands were both Spanish explorers: Alvaro de Mendaña glimpsed Pukapuka in 1595, and in 1606, Pedro Fernández de Quirós stopped at Rakahanga to take on provisions.

In 1773, the English explorer James Cook sighted the islands from his vessel *The Resolution* (among his crew was a young Cornish sailing master by the name of William Bligh, who went on to lead the infamous mutiny aboard *The Bounty* in 1789). Between 1773 and 1777, Cook charted much of the group, and following a fine English tradition of attaching dull, irrelevant names to wonderful places, dubbed the Southern Group islands the 'Hervey Islands' in honour of a Lord of the Admiralty. Fifty years later a Russian cartographer (Admiral Johann von Krusenstern) published the *Atlas de l'Océan Pacifique,* in which he renamed the islands in honour of Captain Cook.

Missionaries

Once the explorers had sailed on to new discoveries (or sticky ends, as was the case with Captain Cook, who was stabbed to death in Hawaii in 1779), it was left to the missionaries to establish long-lasting contact with the people of the Cook Islands. Reverend John Williams of the London Missionary Society (LMS) sailed from Ra'iatea (near present-day Tahiti) to Aitutaki in 1821. There he left two Tahitian preachers, including a newly converted Society Islander named Papeiha. By the time Williams returned two years later, plucky Papeiha had managed to convert practically the entire island, which spurred Williams on to take the gospel to the rest of the Southern Group.

The Cook Islanders probably wished he'd stayed put. For the next 50-odd years, Williams and his Bible-happy followers ruled the islands with an iron rod, imposing a catalogue of draconian doctrines, which even by contemporary standards seemed ridiculously strict, and frequently bordered on the unhinged. Offenders were clobbered with heavy fines, ensuring a steady stream of enforced labour for the missionaries' building projects and a handy source of revenue for the local *riko* (police) and judges.

The influence of the missionaries wasn't all bad, of course. They left the Cook Islanders with some beautiful churches, mostly built from crushed coral and lime, and often intricately decorated with sennit rope and carved wood. Several of the missionaries (especially William Wyatt Gill, a British missionary who spent much of his life on Mangaia) wrote detailed accounts of their experiences, providing a fascinating window onto life in the Cook Islands in the 19th century. But the arrival of the missionaries also spelled the end for many traditional customs in the Cook Islands. The missionaries were keen to suppress the islands' pre-Christian past (especially anything relating to sticky subjects such as ritual sacrifice and cannibalism). Carved idols and hallowed artefacts were burned, *marae* and *paepae* (meeting grounds) were razed to the ground, and many of the old stories and legends were outlawed or forgotten.

Disease, population decline & slave traders

The missionaries brought more than just Christianity and churches to the islands of Polynesia: they inadvertently also brought devastating new diseases, including smallpox and dysentery, the latter of which killed nearly 1000 people in 1830, and caused a drastic population decline across all the islands. To push their cause further, the missionaries cited the mounting death toll as a message from above, and many islanders desperately abandoned their old religion in the hope that they would be spared. But of course, most weren't - as a matter of fact, the population in Rarotonga fell to about one-third within 30 years, and throughout the 19th century deaths exceeded births in the Cook Islands. It wasn't until the early 20th century that the population on Rarotonga began finally to level out, bolstered by migrants from a number of the outer islands.

Disease was not the only thing Cook Islanders had to fear. Brutal Peruvian slave traders, known as blackbirders, took a terrible toll on the Northern Group between 1862and 1863. At first operating as genuine labour recruiters, the traders quickly turned to subterfuge and outright kidnapping to round up their human cargo. Rakahanga and Pukapuka suffered terribly, but

Penrhyn was the blackbirders' main port of call - some estimates reckon that up to three-quarters of the entire population was taken from the island. Few of the 'recruits' ever returned - over 90% died either in transit to Peru or during enforced slave labour.

Protectorate, annexation & independence

The late 19th century saw a headlong rush of colonial expansion over much of the South Pacific. Following several requests for British protection from Makea Takau, the ruling *ariki* of Avarua, Rarotonga was officially made a British overseas protectorate in 1888, mainly in order to avoid a French invasion. The first British Resident (the representative of the British government in a British protectorate) arrived in 1891, but the relationship soon went sour. As a tiny country of little strategic or economic importance, the Cook

Islands held little interest for the British, and following a request from the New ZealandPrime Minister, Richard Seddon, the Cook Islands was annexed to New Zealand in 1901.

The next 50 years were largely quiet ones for the Cook Islands. During WWII the USAbuilt airstrips on Penrhyn and Aitutaki, but the Cooks remained largely untouched by the wider war, unlike many of its neighbours in the South Pacific. In the 1960s, as colonies became increasingly unfashionable, New Zealand leapt at the chance to off-load its expensive overseas dependency and in 1965 the Cook Islands became internally self-governing.

Post-independence politics

The first leader of the newly independent Cook Islands was Albert Henry, leader of the Cook Islands Party (CIP), who had been a prime mover in the push for self-rule, and was the first in a long line of 'colourful' characters in Cook Islands politics. Sir Albert (he was knighted in 1974, as were many of his successors) did much to unify the country in the initial years of independence, but fell spectacularly from grace during the 1978elections, when he became embroiled in a massive scandal involving overseas voters (the CIP flew hundreds of supporters back to the Cook Islands in exchange for a vote in the election, bankrolling the tickets with revenue from the sale of postage stamps by the Cook Islands Philatelic Bureau). The election was handed to the opposition party, the Cook Islands Democratic Party, and Sir Albert was stripped of his knighthood. He died soon after, in 1981; you can see his characteristically ostentatious grave in the Avarua CICC graveyard.

Power seesawed over the ensuing years between the two rival parties, and the political landscape of the period is littered with spats, scandals and larger-than-life personalities - notably Dr Tom Davis, author, canoe-builder and zero-gravity medicine specialist with NASA, and Geoffrey Henry (a cousin of Albert Henry), who only lasted a few months in his first period as leader, but returned as an influential prime minister from 1989 to 1999.

Financial woes

If there's one thing that the Cook Islands have never quite managed to get to grips with, it's balancing the books. In order to finance domestic growth, successive governments were forced to borrow and borrow...and borrow. A series of bad investments (including the massive Sheraton resort on Rarotonga's south coast, which ultimately fell through and left the government about NZ$100 million in debt), and a major scandal involving the country's offshore-banking industry, set the stage for financial meltdown.

In the mid-1990s, foreign debt spiralled out of control, and with bankruptcy looming, the government was forced to take radical action. The economic-stabilisation programme, initiated in 1996, eventually resulted in the sacking of about 2000 government employees - 50% of the public service - a huge proportion of the working population in a country of just 20, 000 inhabitants. Masses of redundant workers left the country in search of jobs elsewhere (mostly to New Zealand or Australia) and never returned, and the country was only saved from the brink thanks to an emergency aid package implemented by the New Zealand government.

Recent history

The Cook Islands still has an eye-watering trade deficit, importing far more than it exports, but thanks to the huge expansion in tourism over recent years, foreign investment is currently flowing into the Cook Islands and keeps the financial wolf from the door. The issue of offshore banking remains a thorny topic; other pressing matters include the ever-accelerating population decline from the outer islands and the gloomy spectre of global warming, which was brought into sharp focus by the unprecedented number of cyclones that swept through the islands in 2005. But it is the implementation of the Unit Titles Act on Rarotonga in 2005 - an act enabling foreigners to lease specific sections of a property in the Cook Islands, rather than the surrounding land - that has really set the cat among the political pigeons. Present prime minister, Jim Marurai, would do well to strap himself in - he looks well and truly set for a bumpy ride.

The roles of *ariki, mataiapo, rangatira* and *tumu korero* survive to the present day. Arguments over who should be holding which title are still as fierce as ever - just check out the daily newspapers

Rarotonga Island

Rarotonga, largest island in the southern group of the Cook Islands, in the South Pacific Ocean about 2,100 miles (3,400 km) northeast of New Zealand. The island is volcanic in origin and has a rugged interior rising to 2,139 feet (652 metres) at Te Manga. Surrounding its mountainous core is a plain, an ancient raised fringing coral reef covered with sediment. The island itself is fringed by a coral reef.

The island was inhabited by Polynesian people around 800 CE and bears marks of a long period of habitation, including marae, or temple platforms, in the valley traversed by Tupapa Stream. The Ara Metua, an ancient pathway, circles the island inland from a paved coastal road. Rarotonga was visited in 1789 by mutineers from the British ship HMS Bounty and was the base from which John Williams of the London Missionary Society (who arrived in 1823) sought to Christianize the islands.

Avarua is the seat of administration for the Cook Islands and the location of a major port. Absence of a suitable lagoon once forced oceangoing ships to lie off the reef and move cargoes ashore via lighters. However, the harbour at Avatiu, to the west of Avarua, has been dredged, and sizable vessels now tie up at the wharf there. Rarotonga's economy is based on citrus fruits, pineapples, coconuts, bananas, and light industry. The tourist industry is a major component of the economy, receiving international tourists at Rarotonga airport. The island has a hospital, Tereora College (a secondary school), and the Cook Islands Tertiary Training Institute, which provides education for careers in trades, technology, and nursing. Area 25.9 square miles (67.1 square km). Pop. (2006) 10,226; (2011) 10,572.

The End